NOURISH

28 DAILY DARES FOR BUSY PEOPLE
CRAVING SUSTAINABLE SELF-CARE

By
Sally Anne Carroll

Sally Anne Carroll / Artisan Communications

www.sallyannecarroll.com

Nourish / Sally Anne Carroll. —1st ed.

ISBN: 979-8-9850671-0-1

Contents

PART

1

INTRODUCTION

Be kinder to yourself. And then let your kindness flood the world.

- Pema Chodron

Whether you are running a business, managing someone else's business, contributing to your office team, running a home, or what have you, ensuring you are cared for and nurtured is critical to your performance. It's critical for your relationships, your energy levels, your brainpower, your stress management, and your health.

When prioritizing your body, mind, spirit, and environment every single day becomes a non-negotiable practice, you can create an unshakeable foundation of well-being that fuels everything that you do. You're more productive. More effective. More creative. More energized. You're less stressed. Less resentful. Less overwhelmed. Overall, you feel a whole lot better.

When you are fully nourished, it becomes less important to do all the things and try to control every external situation to meet your needs. Instead, you know how to meet your core needs on your own and you're doing just that. When you're nourished, you're not cramming your day full and living in overwhelm because your stress is better managed and your head is clearer. You work better, relate better, and lead better *because you feel better*. It really is that simple.

As a life and career coach, I'm a fierce advocate for this level of truly nourishing self-care. I've learned— on my own and through years of working with busy professionals and entrepreneurs—that nourishing ourselves is not a "nice to have." It's critical to our well-being. It really is the fuel that makes everything we do in our personal and professional lives sustainable.

And yet, I hear from too many people that truly nourishing themselves is the first thing that goes out the window when their plates fill up (which is when we need it more than ever!). Since you have this book in your hands, I'm betting you've been there. Maybe you are there right now.

Unfortunately, though, too many of us push away even the most basic of self-care because we're too busy believing and acting as if we have been installed as the CEO of the entire universe and that life as we know it will come to a screeching halt if we take the time to fully invest in our own needs. We put ourselves and our nourishment close to the bottom of our to-do list. We may even harbor hidden (or not so hidden) beliefs that our self-nourishment is not worth the investment. At the root of this are many cultural and societal messages that we may have received, and internalized, over time about the value and necessity of taking time, energy, space, and investment for ourselves.

I want to change that. We *need* to change that, for all of us, and that starts by shifting cultural mindsets that leave our full well-being on the back burner and by making meaningful self-care an integral component of daily life. That mindset is not serving any of us; it's setting a lot of humans up for long-term stress and struggle. It's time to put all of those unhelpful messages on the back burner and embrace a kinder, gentler, and more loving way of being in our lives. We can't fully thrive without a new approach.

Instead, let's reposition self-care as what it truly is: a highly practical and necessary foundation for your life.

Self-nourishment is highly individual and it needs to account for the responsibilities you have and what you know you need in order to show up as your highest self. The practice of nourishing encourages you to tune into yourself and your needs at a deeper level, as well as to start small and experiment with practices that stretch your thinking about how you attend to your body, mind, spirit, and environment. It means integrating a few intentional and well-chosen habits and rituals into your daily life, ones that are intimately tied with what fuels you personally. It's an approach that feels nurturing, fuels energy and is backed up by an increasingly strong body of neuroscience and well-being research. That is what is at the heart of this book and the Nourish challenge.

As you read this book, I want to inspire and challenge you to nourish and energize your mind, body, soul, and environment with practical, proven strategies that are manageable even on the busiest of schedules. This book is designed to help you carve out a little time to check in with yourself and set up a personally meaningful and simple self-care plan that you can implement going forward, and that you can sustain no matter how full life gets.

PART

THE NOURISH CHALLENGE

*Nourishing your whole self so
you can thrive*

What meaningful self-care looks like in your life is up to you, and I hope that this book helps you to answer that question for yourself. How you implement it is based on the responsibilities you have and what you know you need. Think of *Nourish* as your doorway in and your foundation.

Over the next 28 days, I will encourage you to start small and experiment with new practices to take care of your body, mind, spirit, and environment. By the end, you'll have hopefully stretched your thinking about what you need and how you can creatively meet those needs. You'll also integrate a few well-chosen habits and rituals into your daily life. You might find, like I have and many of my clients have, that your investment in even the smallest acts of nourishment pay off in ways you never could have imagined.

A nourished foundation

Meaningful self-care has little to do with luxury, pampering, and indulgence. While I personally enjoy accessing those experiences, too many self-care discussions default to giving ourselves what are essentially delicious treats: massages, mani-pedis, beach vacations, chocolate, eating delicious food, or taking a pocket of time to do that thing we're craving, such as reading a book by the fire or going for a longer-than-usual run. Making time for these fun and pleasurable experiences is important but viewing our self-care through this one-dimensional lens barely scratches the surface of what it means to cultivate meaningful and life-changing ways of being.

Instead, I invite you to commit yourself to a more foundational practice, starting with simple self-care strategies in each of the four key areas of the Nourish challenge: Mind, Body, Spirit, and Environment. This creates an easy and naturally balanced base of individualized self-care, one that is simple to establish and to build upon.

Mind: Nurture a healthy brain and mindset.

Body: Tune into your physical clues, cues, and needs.

Spirit: Fuel for your spiritual and emotional life.

Environment: Create, fine-tune, and commit to a supportive environment.

Can 15 minutes of self-care really make a difference?

Behavioral psychology research has shown that, while larger changes can be hard to make and to stick with, taking smaller, consistent actions repeatedly over time can be highly effective. These smaller commitments, or micro-actions, require little time, effort, and energy and therefore, they're easier to incorporate into your daily schedule. And the more you incorporate them, the more effective they are at creating lasting changes that positively impact your overall self-care. We're employing that science here. You'll take one small action towards deeper self-care every day. Your commitment is 15 minutes. If you want to do more, great. But consistently showing up for yourself every day for a small period of time will start to rewire the changes you want to make and eliminate any time constraints. Everyone can spare 15 minutes.

The Nourish challenge—and this book—is all about taking a stand for nourishing and fueling yourself in meaningful ways. It's also designed with real-life sustainability in mind. That means we will also be incorporating the following guidelines:

Going inward—The Daily Dares are self-guided for an important reason: *understanding what truly nourishes us is an inside job*. I want you to hear your own voice and experiment with what works for you, not somebody else. The goal is for you to listen to your own guidance, adapt what you learn to your life, and find a few practices that will become a natural part of your nourishment routine.

Proven, simple principles—The Daily Dares are designed to be practical, simple actions that can fit into a full schedule. None of the challenges needs to take more than 15 minutes per day, but please spend as much time as you like exploring them. Each one offers evidence- and research-based practices that are well-tested and proven to increase well-being.

Experimentation—Lasting change, the kind that becomes an integral part of your life, happens *through lived experiences*. Be brave enough to try things you haven't tried before. Each of the four sections builds upon each other, creating a solid mind-body-spirit-environment commitment from which you can begin to put your own well-being front and center in your life.

By the end of this book, what I want for you is this:

- Serious progress in taking excellent care of yourself

- Proof that self-care doesn't have to be trivial, difficult, or time-consuming

- Inspiration and commitment to make real self-care part of your routine

- New ideas to manage your energy and refuel your mind, body, and spirit

- Action steps to build a more supportive environment around you

- Firsthand experience of 28 nourishing strategies to adapt to your life

- A simple, personalized, and actionable plan to integrate going forward

At the end of these 28 days, your exploration of what nourishes you will become the basis for a simple and foundational nourishment plan that you can implement right away. Chances are, you'll already be implementing it by the time you finish this book because you'll have found several practices that you want to integrate into your life.

A simple self-care audit

Before we begin, promise yourself that this will not be just another book on the bookshelf, but one that spurs you to take action. You cannot outsource your well-being, and you can't sustainably lead and create in your life when you're not giving yourself what you need to show up at your best. Learning all the strategies in the world will not change anything. Real sustainable change comes from trying something different. It's time to figure out what you need and commit yourself to simple self-care strategies that work for your busy life. This is not a life hack. This is getting real about taking steps to put a solid foundation under everything you do.

Often the first step in nourishing our full well-being is getting clear about where we have not necessarily been doing this. If there are changes that need to be made, now's the time. When assessing your level of self-care, kindness rules, of course, but so does honesty. As you go through this challenge, you may want to record your experiences in a journal or in the spaces provided in this book.

Start with these questions:

What are the self-care practices that truly fuel you?

Where have you neglected or avoided connecting with your mind, body, or spirit?

Where do you need to craft a more supportive environment so that you can feel and be nourished?

What "feel-good" practices are masquerading as (but are not really) self-care?

If your weeks feel draining or cluttered, how are you recharging or "pre-charging" on the weekends?

What fuels and foundations do you need to put into place every week, month, year?

Where are the self-care leaks that need to be plugged?

How can you adjust your daily life to honor a deeper level of self-care?

Think of this as your "before" photo. If you felt truly nourished, what would become possible for you?

What are your intentions and commitments as you begin this book? Take a moment to write them down.

Ready? Let's get going.

FOUNDATION ONE: MIND

*Your mindset matters more
than you know*

How well we take care of ourselves hinges on *how we think about* taking care of ourselves. We all have beliefs, attitudes, assumptions, and unexamined ideas that impact how we nourish our mind, body, and spirit, and how and whether we succeed in building and maintaining supportive environments around us.

Mindset is the first piece of the Nourish foundation because our mindset is pivotal in how we see the situations and circumstances in our lives, make meaning from them and assess what actions we will and won't take as a result. As humans, we are always developing stories and mindsets that drive our behavior and, much of time, we're doing this unawares.

Neuroscience and psychology research are increasingly showing us how we can intentionally rewire how we think and respond, and this week, we're going to start doing just that. Creating a more nourishing mindset (including your mindset about self-care itself) will empower you to engage in more meaningful practices, establish new routines and behaviors, and make transformative and permanent shifts to develop a truly individualized and sustainable commitment to self-care.

We'll be starting off with a clean sweep of our minds because this space clearing alone can have a profound effect on how nourished we feel as we go through our daily lives. The first step towards sustainable self-care starts in your brain. We live in a full and fast-paced world. For many of us, that means we're constantly filling up our minds, both through the intentional taking in of a flow of information and just by virtue of going through the day. When we intentionally engage with our mindset, we give ourselves new power to develop more effective ways of interacting with everything life throws our way.

We will experiment with doing things differently, making different choices, and examining the stories that we live inside of, and that drive our habitual responses. We're going to be exploring proven mindset strategies by trying them on and adjusting them to fit our schedules, needs, and preferences. Each suggested practice, or Daily Dare, builds on the one before it, so I encourage you to be open to trying all of the daily practices as you proceed through this book. Firsthand experience feels so much different than just grasping an idea intellectually, and the results are different too.

Here's where we are headed over the next seven days:

We're going to slow down enough to be aware of what we are thinking, when we are thinking it. This sounds like a simple ask, but on a daily basis, for the majority of us, it simply does not happen. Fifteen minutes is enough time to experience the difference when we slow down and actually hear ourselves think. For many people, this awareness alone, when practiced with grace and compassion, can be the basis of a significant shift in their self-care.

Nothing changes without this awareness of where we are in the present moment. In moments of stillness that is where you can really hear your own wisdom and make choices from an internally driven place instead of from the constant influences of what's happening all around you.

We will also experiment with thinking new thoughts that you've never thought before. When you become more fully aware of what you're thinking, you can more easily adjust that thinking to achieve more desired results. You'll consider what a new perspective might look like and experiment with installing that new storyline in a way that is both believable and authentic to you.

In short, remember this: Busy brains keep us stuck. The first pillar of nourishment starts with clearing out the space so that we can begin to rewire our minds from adversary to ally. Over these seven days, we'll explore several options for repopulating your clearer mind with nourishing thoughts and practices.

Each day, there will be a new Daily Dare to try, all of which are designed to help you gently set aside any thoughts that have kept you from establishing an ingrained habit of meaningful self-care and start replacing them with a more nourishing mindset.

As the late Wayne Dyer famously said, "When you change the way you look at things, what you look at changes."

5 NOURISHING MINDSET SHIFTS TO CONSIDER THIS WEEK

I am present enough to notice and name how I'm thinking.

I am willing to experiment with new thoughts and ideas.

I can harness the science of optimism and positivity to enhance my experience.

It is possible to clear out space in my busy brain.

I choose constructive compassion towards myself.

Daily Dare #1:
Choose another thought

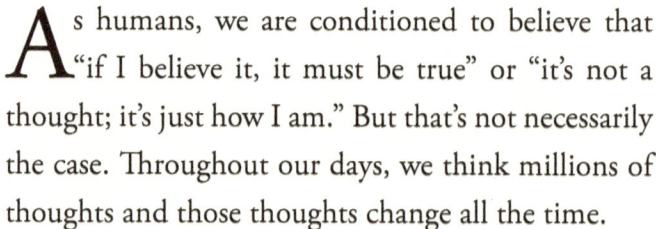

As humans, we are conditioned to believe that "if I believe it, it must be true" or "it's not a thought; it's just how I am." But that's not necessarily the case. Throughout our days, we think millions of thoughts and those thoughts change all the time.

We don't have to think any of them.

We all have examples where new evidence has changed our thinking about a topic, an opinion we once held, or a circumstance.

What is true is that most of us don't spend a whole lot of time objectively looking at what we're thinking unless something comes along that causes us to question that thinking. And while challenging our thoughts is... well, challenging... it's a lot more challenging to nourish ourselves well and built a sustainable, thriving life on a foundation of decidedly *un-nourishing* thoughts.

How we think has direct impacts on how we feel, and the emotions that we're feeling (or trying not to feel) flow on to influence the actions that we take, the way we behave, and the things we avoid doing or procrastinate.

So, let's begin with bringing more awareness to how you think about self-care and creating sustainable balance and nourishment into your daily life. Explore the connections between what you tell yourself about self-care and the results that you're seeing. Remember, those thoughts are optional. So, be sure to choose the ones that are most likely to lead to the actions you want to take.

Your 15-minute challenge:

Write down the top five thoughts you have about self-care, nourishing yourself, and creating sustainable balance in your life. Do you believe it's difficult? Fun? Impossible? Important? That you're already doing what you know to do?

Now, write down *how you feel* whenever you dwell on those top five thoughts. What *actions or behaviors* naturally follow when you're dwelling on those thoughts and feeling that way?

That's it. As you notice these thoughts come up, try to practice refining or reframing them as needed over the next 28 days.

What I believe about self-care:

As a result, I feel, think and do the following:

Daily Dare #2:
Prove a better story

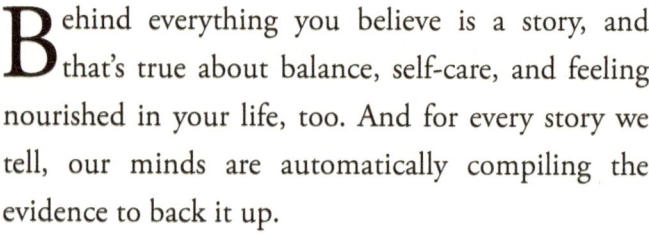

Behind everything you believe is a story, and that's true about balance, self-care, and feeling nourished in your life, too. And for every story we tell, our minds are automatically compiling the evidence to back it up.

The quality of that story and the evidence that you're using to support it are going to directly influence how you feel, the actions you're taking, and all of the results that you experience. The thing is, though, stories are a dime a dozen. There are plenty of them out there.

Think about one obstacle that keeps coming up for you around taking really good care of yourself. Maybe it's that you can't get to the gym, but you feel like you need that. Maybe it's the time demands of your crazy boss. Maybe deep down you're not feeling like you deserve extra self-care time. It doesn't matter what it is; we're going to look at it from a few different perspectives.

If you were an impartial observer of this experience, you might notice different aspects of this situation than the way you initially thought of it above. Someone who has overcome that obstacle themselves might see it differently. A person who might benefit from you achieving what you want could have an entirely new perspective, whereas someone who might not could view it differently again.

Today's strategy is simple: You can pile up the evidence in support of a story that holds you back from what you want to create or you can pile it up in support of the story that empowers you to create what you want. Your choice.

Your 15-minute challenge:

Today, find some evidence that the story you thought of when reading this is true. Yes, that thing is certainly going to stop you from the outcome that you want to create.

When you're done, find some evidence that this obstacle is completely surmountable. Who do you know of that has done or is doing what you would like to be doing? Maybe you've got a track record a mile long in making things happen, but you haven't put that skill to work on your self-care. Maybe you just need a plan or additional support.

Which evidence would you like to believe? Write a one-sentence story to support the evidence you choose.

_____

_____

_____

_____

_____

_____

_____

_____

_____

_____

_____

Daily Dare #3:
Find something right

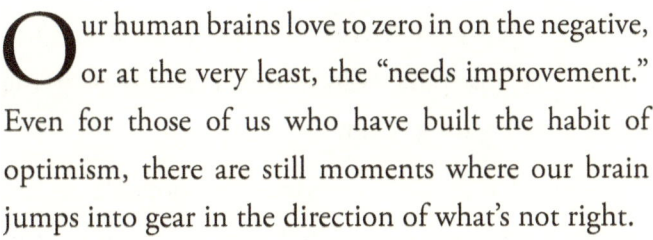

Our human brains love to zero in on the negative, or at the very least, the "needs improvement." Even for those of us who have built the habit of optimism, there are still moments where our brain jumps into gear in the direction of what's not right.

As noted psychologist Rick Hanson has said, our brains tend to be like "Velcro for the bad and Teflon for the good." That's because we're human, and our human brains have developed to respond more strongly to negative stimuli and to default to a negative bias. In other words, on autopilot, we can tend to be more motivated by negative information, use it as a decision-making criterion, and be more sensitive to negative input from others.

We can, however, practice turning this around. We can build the habit of finding what's right in any situation, reframe our thinking and refocus our thoughts on more positive inputs. Over time, this can be a transformative practice and can rewire our brain to establish new patterns of thinking. For example, research on the emotion of gratitude, the actions we can take to create it, and the impacts on well-being have born this out time and again. But before gratitude, there is approval. It's hard to feel grateful when your attention is always on what's not right. That just puts us in a constant cycle of trying to fix what's wrong. Ugh.

Consider this: What would be possible if you created a cycle of approval in your own life? What can you find right with your life as it is right now? What can you find right with your boss, your partner, your children, your job, your schedule, your body?

Focusing on what's right doesn't mean you don't want more or even that there aren't things you may want to change. It means that you're starting from what's right instead of focusing on what's wrong. That's a much more effective and fun way to build something even better.

Your 15-minute challenge:

Today, take five minutes at the start of your day to find something that's right. What do you approve of right now?

At the end of your day, do it again.

For extra challenge and impact, try practicing this whenever you're feeling stressed, annoyed, or tired.

Daily Dare #4:
Focus on what you're creating

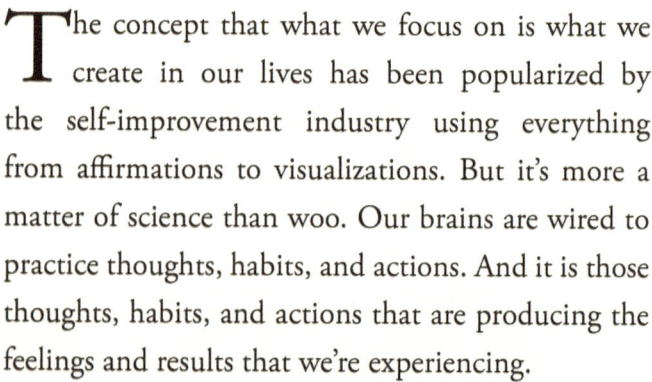

The concept that what we focus on is what we create in our lives has been popularized by the self-improvement industry using everything from affirmations to visualizations. But it's more a matter of science than woo. Our brains are wired to practice thoughts, habits, and actions. And it is those thoughts, habits, and actions that are producing the feelings and results that we're experiencing.

The reticular activating system, a bundle of nerves located at the brain stem that governs our wake/sleep cycle and serves as the brain's attention center, is a part of this complex system. Part of its role is to filter attention and organize information around what is relevant to us.

It's often cited as a reason that we tend to gravitate towards seeing evidence for what we already believe, and why once you've purchased a black Jeep Wrangler you start seeing them everywhere (true story!).

In other words, you are creating your experience all the time. You are, essentially, always in a position of choice. That's an empowering place to be. It does, though, take active practice to continually stop, check in, and ask yourself how you're using that power of choice and what focus instructions you're giving to your mind. Retraining your brain to respond to new stimuli doesn't happen overnight. But it does shift over time, and when your practice inevitably produces results, then it really starts to shift.

Evidence is a powerful motivator. Consider your mental focus as a tool that you can put to use however will best serve what you're trying to achieve.

If you want to create a better balance between your personal and work lives, what do you need to be focused on to create that? (Hint: reading or talking about how balance is a myth will *never* get you there.) If wellness is your goal, are you focused on thoughts and actions that help you achieve wellness? Or something else?

Practice checking in with your focus and adjusting as necessary and you will experience the truth of "what you focus on expands."

Your 15-minute challenge:

Check in with yourself three times during the next 24 hours and ask yourself this:

How is what I am doing right now connected to what I am creating in my life? Is that what I want to be creating? Or is there a disconnect? What, if anything, do I need to shift about my intent and focus to create a more nourishing experience?

Daily Dare #5:
Listen

One of the biggest red flags that I hear when I talk to clients who are overwhelmed, stressed, and feeling like they need to get a better handle on taking care of themselves is this:

I can't even hear myself think.

Who hasn't been there?

When we cannot hear ourselves think, then our attention becomes easy prey to the external world. We succumb to doing and saying what's easiest right now, even when it isn't nourishing. This is a key part of how we say yes to obligations when what we really want to say is no. We succumb to listening to the imagined voices of inner critics and/or the real voices of other people around us. What we don't hear is our own wisdom or intuitive nudges. We lose touch with the deep knowing that is under the surface.

This is why it can be so effective for a healthy mindset to cultivate listening practices as a part of our self-care routines. Taking the time to listen allows us to go deeper within ourselves and sort out what is truly nourishing for us and what is extraneous. Listening more intentionally can also better connect our mind to our body, to what we're feeling emotionally and physically, and to what we truly desire but haven't spoken out loud. Here are a few ideas to try:

- Meditate with your breath, a mantra, or a short, guided meditation. Notice what comes up during that time.

- Use the athlete's practice of visualization. What would you like your inner wisdom to weigh in on? Close your eyes and imagine that conversation.

- Get in the shower, on your bike, out in the garden, in the car—wherever it is that you "have the best ideas." Pay attention to the ideas that come up for you in this space.

Your 15-minute challenge:

Listen deeply to yourself and allow your mindset to be nourished by what comes to you. Choose a listening practice that invites your inner wisdom to show itself. Practice it for 15 minutes today.

Daily Dare #6:
Create white space

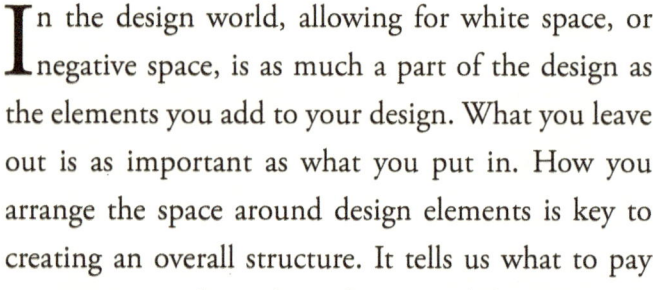

In the design world, allowing for white space, or negative space, is as much a part of the design as the elements you add to your design. What you leave out is as important as what you put in. How you arrange the space around design elements is key to creating an overall structure. It tells us what to pay attention to and avoids confusion and clutter.

It's the same in our daily lives. When our heads are filled with information, activities, plans, and to-do lists, our brains can easily become overloaded, crowded, and cluttered. The result? We're frazzled. Unclear. Irritable. Burned out.

Designers consciously use white space to achieve their vision. That includes actively creating and arranging white space, as well as leveraging the naturally occurring (passive) space that occurs between the shapes, lines, and letters of a design.

We can do the same for our brains by intentionally carving out more space for ourselves between the ongoing activity of our lives. We can create mental space by letting go of the noise and the distraction, even for short periods of time. We can use the little pockets of space that naturally show up in our days, not for squeezing more in, but for leaving something out.

We all need white space in our lives to thrive.

Your 15-minute challenge:

Where do you need more white space in your life? Call a quick date with your calendar and do these three things:

- Add a 10-minute buffer around scheduled meetings or activities. Block out that time.

- Cancel one event or commitment that you are not fully invested or engaged in doing.

- Decide where you can carve out a daily 10-minute pocket of time for breathing space. It can be in the morning, before bed, between meetings, at lunch. You can sit quietly, meditate, or simply do nothing but enjoy the space.

Daily Dare #7:
Edit your attention

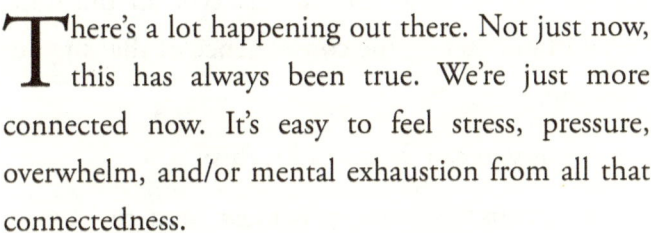

There's a lot happening out there. Not just now, this has always been true. We're just more connected now. It's easy to feel stress, pressure, overwhelm, and/or mental exhaustion from all that connectedness.

I hear this especially when I speak to my clients and when I engage on social media. We swim in a never-ending stream of suggestions of what we should be paying attention to, what we should be doing, what we should not be doing, and which larger conversations we should be having. We hear about how we should and should not be running our lives, our careers, and our businesses.

A little reality check here:

You can't participate in all the important conversations, all the time. Not constructively.

You can't keep up with all the news, all the time. Not healthfully.

You can't donate and volunteer to all the causes, all the time. Not sustainably.

You can't take all the actions, be at all the places, be aware and plugged in to all the issues, please all the people, learn all the things. Not all the time, not without feeling the consequence of that in your own life.

What you can do instead is this:

- Focus on where you most want to have an impact.

- Limit conversations that deplete you.

- Choose intentionally.

- Contribute effectively.

- Trust yourself to know where and how that is.

- Lead in your own life.

- Add as you have the capacity, necessity, desire, and inspiration.

Be willing to say an enlightened no so that you can say yes in a way that is sustainable, effective, and nourishing for your whole life.

Your 15-minute challenge:

Clear your mind by focusing on what truly matters to you right now. Here are a few places to start:

- What can you do in the next 15 minutes to remove distractions that are not serving you?

- If you're active in larger conversations (politics, community, activism, education, social justice), choose the one area that feels most important to you right now and focus your attention and energy there.

- Choose another place to say an enlightened no, so that you can say yes to your life.

Places to say no

Places to focus

FOUNDATION TWO: BODY

Fine-tuning your machine

When most of us think about taking good care of ourselves, we jump right to our body. It stands to reason that we think of our bodies as ground zero for good self-care. After all, we live in these bodies every day. No one else is going to take care of them for us.

But more often than not, we also jump immediately to the things that we're *not* doing but think we "should" be doing. Eating the superfoods and meditating and implementing the latest exercise study and the science on sleep.

Often, what I hear goes something like this: "I know I need to get more exercise, eat a better diet, get more sleep. I need to drink less. Lose weight." In other words, the concept of self-care has just gone from nourishing yourself to tacking a whole bunch of daily mandates onto your already lengthy to-do list. Instead of nourishing the body, the focus is too often on guilt, discipline, willpower, and living up to external ideals.

That's not nourishing and it's not motivating.

Alternately, we might think of self-care as pampering ourselves because "we deserve it" for having battled stress all week. You know, scheduling a massage, getting a pedicure, heading to a spa, sleeping in, treating ourselves to a special meal or favorite food or a glass of wine.

Meaningful physical self-care doesn't start from either of those places, though it could include any and all of those activities. It's more about practice and care, and easy habits that build on each other until they're part of a healthy lifestyle.

The next foundation of your Nourish challenge is designed to help you connect more to your body so that you can let go of all the shoulds and fall in love with caring for your physical body from a place of "feel-good." Your way.

Your body is where you live every day. It's up to you to decide how you want it to feel and perform. It's up to you to notice what fuels it and what does not. When you start adding and subtracting practices with that knowing, now you're effectively nourishing your body. You'll soon find that even a couple of well-chosen practices will have a dramatically positive effect.

So over the next seven days, we're going to explore and experiment with activities and habits that science has proven to be good for our human bodies. But we're throwing out all the rules of how they need to look in your life. I invite you to use each of the Daily Dares as an opportunity to have fun with the many ways that you can nourish and feel great in your physical body. I encourage you to approach each day with a spirit of play and an attitude of "I get to" rather than "I have to." Because if nourishing your body doesn't feel good and fit your unique circumstances, you aren't going to stick with it. And we are all about creating sustainable ways to nourish the body that fit how we really live.

Here's what you'll be up to this week:

You're going to keep slowing down, enough to feel your body and the feedback that it's giving you. As we learned over the last seven days, we don't do this with our brains nearly enough. Many people do it even less with their bodies because so many of us are always stuck in our heads!

When you pay attention to your body, you might be surprised at what feels good to you and what doesn't. ("One more" glass of wine, I am looking at you.) You're also going to set aside all of the rules, all of the musts, all of the conflicting health headlines and body hack social media influencer posts. Don't worry if you miss keeping on top of it all; you can do that when your Nourish challenge is over. I doubt you'll want to, though.

You'll be focused all week on simple, implementable practices that are proven help you to physically manage your energy and care for your body. So, while you'll be asked to experiment with new activities, ideas, and commitments, this is not the time to be setting stretch goals or worrying about how to motivate yourself. Each of the seven Daily Dares are designed to support you in creating daily self-care rituals that build on themselves over time.

As the ancient Chinese philosopher Zhuang Zhou wisely suggested, when you take care of your body, the rest will become stronger, too.

5 NOURISHING BODY PRACTICES TO CONSIDER THIS WEEK

I am letting go of other people's rules about how I should eat and move.

I pay close attention to what my body is asking for throughout the day.

I continually carve out small pockets of time for rest and renewal.

I ask myself what feels most loving and nurturing in the moment and just do that.

I slow down and inhabit my body rather than staying in my head or my favorite escapes.

Daily Dare #8:
Eat for fuel + pleasure

❧

What we put into our bodies has a huge impact on how we feel, think, and function every day. Fueling our physical bodies with the nutrients it needs is a critical part of meaningful grown-up self-care.

But it also feels like there's another rule every day about what we should—and should not—eat for well-being. And while there may be some tried and tested rules of thumb (vegetables are nutrient-dense and good for us, and fries every night won't make us feel great), so much of what passes for dietary advice is just a sales pitch or simplified reporting on a complex small group research study.

True self care—really fueling our bodies through healthy nutrition—requires a letting go of this, and it requires us to tune into our bodies so that we can learn from them and fuel them in a way that is satisfying and sustainable.

Today, we're letting go of "how I should eat" rules. We are letting go of the mindset that this food is "good" and that food is "bad" and that we must deprive ourselves or pay the piper. And we are letting go of any judgments that we are "being good" or "being bad" when we are making a food choice.

Food is simply food. Some of it is incredibly healthy for our cells and makes us feel good from the inside out. Some is not. Some may have other intangible benefits. Sometimes we need a healthy dose of greens, and sometimes, a really delicious chocolate chip cookie will feed our souls. Self-care is about balance. It's about learning to feed ourselves, fully.

Experiment with listening to your body and eating what fuels you. Eat what feels like pleasure— true pleasure, not empty filling up a hole or plugging your emotions kind of pleasure. You can feel the difference.

Be mindful of what goes into your body today. Notice your food with all your senses. When you eat, fuel *your whole self.* Just for today, give it a try.

Over time, this one simple habit will help you to let go of any drama around dietary choices, find the way of eating that your body responds best to, and stay consistent with what works for you.

Your 15-minute challenge:

Pick one of these practices to try on for today:

- Have that food you dearly love but never allow yourself. Eat it slowly and without guilt.

- Choose the lunch that makes you feel truly nourished and healthy.

- Replace one food that doesn't make you feel good with one that does.

- Ditch the food you only eat because you read somewhere that it's healthy. There are plenty of healthy foods to choose from; pick one that you find delicious instead.

Daily Dare #9:
Move in a way that feels good

How do you feel about exercise? Is it a stress reliever in your life or a stress inducer? Do you relish your workouts and feel like they're an integral part of your week? Are you following a rigid program that feels like a must-do even though it bores you to tears?

Are you beating yourself up because you didn't get to the gym this week—or any week? Are you pushing yourself too far, too fast, trying to keep up with the latest weight loss fad? There are no right answers here. Most of us have inhabited a variety of beliefs and behaviors when it comes to the role of exercise in our lives. But there's no room left to argue that healthy movement doesn't benefit our bodies. It does. The science is in.

While we often think of exercise as related to weight loss, that is not the point here. Regular activity improves our health and well-being. It extends our longevity. It positively influences our stress levels, our hormones, our mood, how well we carry out the activities of our day, and how we feel in our bodies every day.

Today, I invite you to put aside your views of how you should be exercising or how you usually exercise. Instead, make a commitment to incorporate some movement into your day, but not just your usual movement. Choose movement that feels *great* to you. Even if you love your regular exercise routine, I encourage you to try something different to mix it up. You can add to your usual routine if you don't want to disrupt your exercise schedule, or you can substitute one activity for another.

When we switch things up for our bodies, we can better sense how they want and need to move. Our bodies were made to be *active*, not necessarily to kill it at the gym every day and not necessarily to sit all day long without breaks. Pay attention and follow the ideas that come up for you.

Your 15-minute challenge:

To get yourself moving in a more intuitive, nourishing, and consistent way, try this:

- Do a seven-minute workout in the morning before work.

- Use dumbbells between video conferences or walk while on a long phone call.

- Try sprinting with your favorite activity.

- Stop what you're doing and stretch your body with a few simple yoga poses.

- Switch up your gym routine by adding a new challenging activity.

- Get outside and play.

- Be creative and just move. Do this in a way that feels delicious and fun.

Daily Dare #10:
Real rest

Rest. We all need it, but many of us are not getting enough of it. In fact, when you have a busy schedule with a plate full of commitments and obligations, rest can seem like a luxury. "I'll sleep when I'm dead" is a dangerous mantra.

The reality is, though, is that we are in charge of those calendars and those commitments and carving out time for rest and renewal is just not optional if we want our bodies to work properly. And yet, we persist.

Our physical and mental health depends on restful practices such as getting a healthy amount and quality of sleep, managing our stressors, and taking time out from constant busy-ness. More and more, we are seeing cultural shifts towards prioritizing those parts of our life not because it's trendy, but because we must. Self-reported feelings of burnout are at epidemic levels in part because we have become so used to continually doing and not having time for rest and renewal.

Imagine, what would real rest look and feel like to you? More importantly, what would be different in your life if you were feeling rested?

One of the things I personally find nourishing is having a yoga practice, so one way that I have always worked real rest into my day is by enjoying 10 minutes of a restorative yoga pose. When my schedule included long workdays with a 90-minute commute, I savored this as soon as I arrived home. These days, I enjoy doing a short rest practice before bed or enjoying restorative classes online or at my local yoga studio.

Where can you carve out a few minutes in your calendar to give yourself this necessary gift? You're going to experiment with that.

Your 15-minute challenge:

Today, add 15 minutes of real rest to your day. Choose any way of resting that feels natural and nourishing to you. Here are some simple ideas you could try:

- Sneak in a 15-minute nap.

- Take a break to sit quietly in nature.

- Enjoy a short breathing or guided meditation in the middle of the day.

- Plan to go to sleep 10 minutes earlier.

- Set your alarm for 10 minutes later. Don't hit snooze, that's not restful!

- Schedule a respite for yourself where you can fully rest for an hour, a day, or a weekend.

Daily Dare #11:
Meet your breath

❧

The most elemental part of our body is our breath. We take in around 23,000 of them every single day. Yet, many of us routinely hold our breath or breathe shallowly. As a result, we don't allow our bodies and brains to fully oxygenate through the lungs. That's a lot of wasted breath!

We've become so used to breathing in a shallow way, holding our stomachs in and not fully expanding our lungs, that for many of us, deep breathing feels forced and even unnatural. Deep abdominal breathing allows our bodies to take in the oxygen they need and to release carbon dioxide.

It may seem simple, but deep belly breathing, in which we can feel our chest and belly expand with breath, is a profound way to nourish the body. It's one of the most powerful things that we can do every day, and it costs us nothing.

You might find it helpful to put your hand on your belly to physically feel how this type of breathing works. Once you're used to practicing it in a focused way, you can easily call up a few deep breaths throughout your day or whenever you're feeling stressed.

Deep breathing can calm us down by slowing the heart and stabilizing blood pressure. It can help us manage nervous tension and anxiety. It improves digestion. Studies have shown that this type of focused breathing can improve our immune system, relax our physical stress responses, and even improve our sleep.

Your 15-minute challenge:

Practice slow and focused abdominal breathing. Here's a simple exercise to try:

Sit or lie down in a quiet place. Breathe normally for a few seconds without trying to control your breath. Then deepen your breath by inhaling slowly through your nose. As you fill your lungs, let your chest and belly expand. Hold that breath for a count of three. Now, exhale slowly through your nose or your mouth, fully emptying your breath and deflating your belly and chest. Repeat for eight rounds, consciously taking in deep breaths and letting them go.

Daily Dare #12:
Love your real body

❧

I have yet to meet anyone without a solid self-care practice who doesn't tell me about the things they dislike about their body. This antagonistic relationship with our physical selves feels crazy when you think about it, and it's also incredibly common. We're socialized to hold ourselves up to physical ideals instead of to appreciate the beauty and performance of the physical machines that we inhabit every day.

Our bodies are amazing. Think, for a minute, about everything your body does for you every single day. Our livers filter out toxins and perform 500 different functions every day. Sensory messages fly from our fingers to our brains at 125 mph. Our eyes can distinguish between a million different colors. You get the point.

You may want to build muscle or lose fat, be uncomfortable with a changing or aging body, or want to alter something about your appearance. That's fine if it is coming from a place of love. *This* is the miraculous body you have been given. Habits are healthiest and easiest to sustain when they come from a place of authentic appreciation and wanting to make something good even better. If you contrast that with struggling to fix what you perceive as wrong and grasping for arbitrary and external ideals, well, there's no contest here about what is more nourishing, healthy, or motivating.

Your body powers you through your busy days, weeks, years, and decades. Appreciate it and treat it with more love, care, and nourishment. Every single day, starting right now. You may not fall in love with your perceived flaws overnight. Let's be real. It takes time to overcome all that conditioning. But why not try to embrace all of you and see where that takes you?

Your 15-minute challenge:

Today, try something along these lines:

- Do something nourishing for the part of your body you love the most.

- Take tender loving care of the part of your body that you're least fond of.

- Lovingly massage your skin with oil before your shower, or lotion afterwards.

- Look at yourself naked and thank your glorious body for all that it manages to do each day.

- Make a gratitude list for your body so that you have a go-to resource the next time you become focused on wanting to change it.

- Smile at yourself in the mirror and take the time to really see yourself.

Daily Dare #13:
Less is more

So much of the traditional view of self-care is that it's about adding things to your schedule, doing more and doing better. Sometimes, though, what's really called for is to subtract, eliminate and *do less*.

Now that you've spent a few days tuning into how you eat, move, sleep, breathe, and appreciate your body, you might already have a few thoughts about what your body needs *less* of. As you've listened more closely, you might have received clear messages from your body about what it doesn't need.

If reading this brings something to mind right away, go with that. Your first thought is often your best thought when it comes to nourishing your body. If nothing comes to mind, then today is the day to think about letting go of non-nourishing habits.

Would your body function well with less of a certain food or food group, or maybe less food overall? Less caffeine, less alcohol? Is there a habit that it's time to let go of or trade for something that increases your energy? Are you hitting your workouts so hard that your hormones are becoming depleted?

Too much of anything leads to overwhelm, not nourishment. That goes for food, drink, exercise, sleep, so-called optimal self-care routines, you name it. What can you use less of? Just let it go.

Your 15-minute challenge:

It's time to take something off your plate, so that you can free up room for a more nourishing option. Here are a few ideas but listen to your gut on this one, as you know what your body is loving and what it's not:

- Swap out a coffee for another drink that fuels you.

- Drop a food that you know isn't working for you.

- Let go of an activity that you're only doing because you think it's good for you.

- Jot down a quick plan to get back to basics, starting today.

- Commit to scale back where you know you're overdoing it.

- Exchange exercise you don't love for exercise that you do love and schedule it in.

Daily Dare #14:
Tune in to tune up

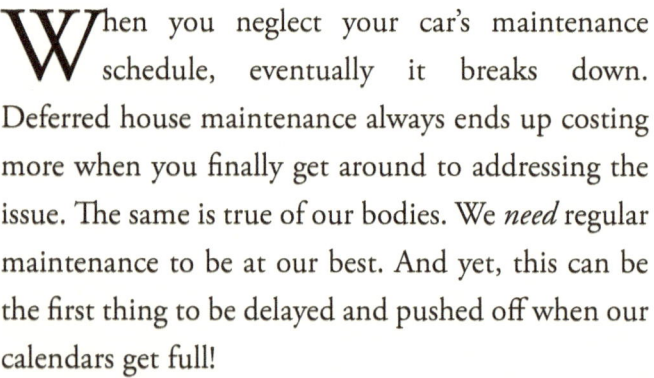

When you neglect your car's maintenance schedule, eventually it breaks down. Deferred house maintenance always ends up costing more when you finally get around to addressing the issue. The same is true of our bodies. We *need* regular maintenance to be at our best. And yet, this can be the first thing to be delayed and pushed off when our calendars get full!

Creating a foundation of regular physical maintenance actually streamlines your self-care practice. It allows you to seamlessly take care of routine upkeep and reap the benefits of a well-performing body. Think of this practice as scheduling regular tune-ups for your body.

A tune-up can include anything from stocking your home each week with the foods you choose to prepare and eat to regularly scheduling preventative medical and dental care. It might mean scheduling physically nourishing habits such as stretching every morning or walking for 30 minutes every day. It could include your routines for taking care of your skin and hair, ongoing bodywork appointments, or something else that continually nourishes your physical body and keeps it in good working order.

How can you create a foundation of ongoing maintenance for your body? Today, you'll take a few minutes to do—or decide on and schedule—a tune-up.

Your 15-minute challenge:

Give your body the regular servicing it needs:

- Schedule a medical check-up.

- Schedule your dental or eye exams.

- Attend to what needs attending to—what have you been putting off?

- Consider a massage, acupuncture, chiropractic, or other bodywork.

- Write out a healthy meal plan for the week.

- Stock up on your favorite body care essentials so that you're never without.

- Add a few minutes of stretching to your morning or evening routine.

FOUNDATION THREE: SPIRIT

Heeding the call of your spirit

What's calling for deep attention in your life? What brings you unfettered joy? What helps you to stay emotionally resilient through life's challenges? Understanding and articulating the answers to these questions is the essence of hearing and feeding your spirit, so that you have the emotional energy you need to function at a high level throughout your life.

Many of us, when we think of what feeds our soul and spirit, might point to time spent living consciously, paying mindful attention to the present moment, investing in personal growth, deepening our faith practices, or immersing ourselves in the awe of nature. It can be challenging to describe exactly what feeds you on a spiritual level or why, but we often know the felt sense of it. It's that thing that energizes you and makes you feel both alive and deeply rooted. You can feel the absence when it's missing.

You might find that your inner spirit soars when participating in your chosen religious practices, reading spiritual texts, or engaging with a faith community or other group that defines belonging for you. It might be that getting up early and walking silently through your neighborhood infuses your spirit at the start of your day. Perhaps it's making time to laugh or play with your family and friends or to hike into a breathtaking wilderness area. It might be sacred time set aside for creating art or quietly reading a book of poetry.

When it comes to the things that fuel you on spiritual level, there are no right answers or must-dos. There is only coming home to yourself consistently enough and quietly enough to feel those places of true connection. That's why, for the next seven days, we are going to dive into a variety of areas, and we're going to start with reconnecting to yourself when you are at your best and experiencing life at your most grounded place.

First, you will identify your own personal standards, the ones that you live by now and any new ones that you want to set for your life at this point in time. Knowing what energizes or drains your spirit is the perfect starting point for recharging and plugging back into the wisest, most intuitive part of yourself.

You'll also explore six other practices, each one founded in research on well-being and flourishing. During each of these seven days, you will be asked to pay close attention to what your spirit is calling for and offer it up to yourself. You will stretch your courage capacity with a little healthy risk-taking. You'll harness the incredible power of positivity as connected to your emotions and allow yourself to find inspiration and true awesomeness. You'll also decide to be incredibly good to yourself, while also stepping up your game when it comes to connecting with the people who are most important in your life. Taking the time to fill yourself up—even through 15-minute actions—allows us to connect to others in more authentic and empathetic ways, further nourishing the spirit.

By the end of this week, you will have experimented with seven ways to feed your spirit and fill your soul. We are all highly individual in terms of the types of activities and environments that we find fulfilling in this way so, as always, please use the examples given as a starting point and follow your wise intuition about how you can personalize and make each day meaningful for you.

Each of the Spirit Daily Dares is chosen to help you tap into the wellspring of soul energy inside you and connect more deeply to yourself and to the larger world. In the words of the Buddha, just as a candle cannot burn without fire, men cannot live without a spiritual life. Whatever that means to you, it's key to feeling nourished.

5 SOUL-FILLING PRACTICES TO
CONSIDER THIS WEEK

I remember who I am and what truly matters to me.

*I am willing to find out what fuels me and do
more of that.*

I connect to something that is larger than me.

I experiment with feeling however I feel in the moment.

*I create tiny but non-negotiable routines that
fill my spirit.*

Daily Dare #15:
Set your standards

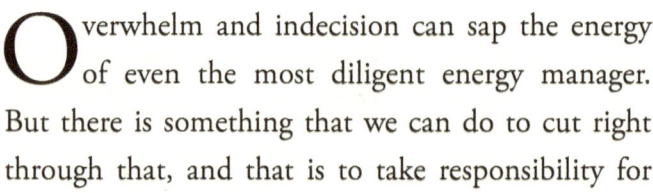

Overwhelm and indecision can sap the energy of even the most diligent energy manager. But there is something that we can do to cut right through that, and that is to take responsibility for setting personal standards that nourish us.

Setting your standards is always about you and nobody else. It's entirely about what you do and don't do, what you choose to have and not have in your life. When you become incredibly clear and make a conscious choice to raise your standards to a level that feels really good, that is the definition of deep self-care.

Think about this for a moment. If you connect to the heart of what truly matters to you, what guides you through tough times and motivates you in good times? How are you behaving when you feel your best? What's surrounding you and what are you making time for? For example, what would it mean if your standard is that you don't tolerate drama from yourself or anyone else? What if your standard was that you are a person who eats well and exercises? It's not a "have-to." It's just what you do.

These "rules for yourself" grow and evolve as you do and they will reflect the season of life that you're in. The point is, they're always your choice and there's always room to nudge your standards closer to your vision for who you are and how you want to live.

This dare might feel challenging for you before it feels nourishing. That's the case for many of us, but I promise that if you take it on and get serious about practicing your new standards, it will be a game changer. Not just for deepening your level of self-care, but for improving your daily life experience.

Your 15-minute challenge:

What comes to mind when you think about the principles that guide you? Make a list of the ones that you'd love to incorporate more of every day.

Notice how you feel when you look at this list. Where do you feel resistance? Where do you feel resonance? How can you honor these principles that matter to you even more every day?

Finish these sentences:

I am a person who _____ .

I am a person who does not _____ .

_____ is non-negotiable for me.

What matters to me that I make time every day/week for _____ .

Personal standards:

_____

_____

_____

_____

_____

_____

_____

_____

Daily Dare #16:

Honor your cravings

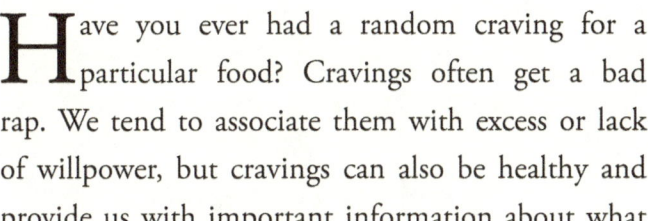

Have you ever had a random craving for a particular food? Cravings often get a bad rap. We tend to associate them with excess or lack of willpower, but cravings can also be healthy and provide us with important information about what our mind and body need.

When I was younger, my mother always advised eating a food if I was craving it. Not to excess, of course. That's not really satisfying a craving; overindulging is something else entirely. Her reasoning was that if we are craving a food, it must have something that our body needs in that moment. I've found this to be true for me. I've had several doctors dispense this advice as well.

Sometimes it's a vitamin or mineral, or the hydration of a water-rich food like a green juice or a melon that my body wants. Or it might be a taste experience like a rich cheese. Sometimes, food is more about feeding the spirit than the body.

Honoring cravings in other areas of my life has been a simple self-care practice I've had for years. Some days, I notice that I am craving a little more rest; on others, I crave the energetic release of movement and stretching. Sometimes, the craving is for a looser weekly schedule than is the norm.

Listen in and see what your spirit craves today. Honor that.

Your 15-minute challenge:

Sit with your cravings for 15 minutes to see what bubbles up for you. Where can you honor that craving and give yourself a little piece of it now? It doesn't need to be all or nothing:

- If you crave a vacation, how can you create a mini respite, day trip, or a day off?

- If you crave peace and quiet, how can you honor that in this moment?

- Do you long for an adventure?

- Are you missing your favorite creative outlets?

- Maybe you need to shift gears and prioritize a little fun or social time?

Cravings	How to enjoy it now

Daily Dare #17:
Be awed and inspired

It's been said that we are all spiritual beings having a human experience. I believe this to be true. No matter how you feed or express yourself spiritually, we all need that deeper level of meaning and connection to something larger than ourselves to thrive.

Studies show that people who regularly experience a feeling of awe are more satisfied with their lives overall, more charitable, and are often healthier because their bodies have lower inflammation and manage stress better.

The good news is that we don't have to wait for inspiration to strike or for awesome events to happen to us. We can create those experiences and cultivate the feelings for ourselves.

Some of the ways that researchers have done this with their test subjects is to have them watch an awe-inspiring video, read inspirational texts, or journal in detail about a memory of feeling awed or connected to something larger than themselves. Traveling to a beautiful place, a walk in the forest, a church sermon, volunteer opportunities, watching your garden change over time—all of these have the potential to connect you to a sense of something larger.

There are many ways that you can cultivate a feeling of awe, inspiration, or spiritual connection in your life. What's more, when we're feeling inspired or awed, time can often seem to expand. So, if you've ever wished for more time in your life, today's Dare is perfect for you.

Your 15-minute challenge:

Spend 15 minutes today immersing yourself in something that inspires you, connects you to larger purpose, or invokes a sense of awe within you.

If you want to go further, create at least one place to collect items that inspire you or brainstorm practices that you could do every day to connect you to that feeling. Be sure to jot down a few notes about what you notice afterwards.

Daily Dare #18:
Stand with yourself

———
❧

Sometimes we do not believe in ourselves. Sometimes we secretly believe we don't measure up. Instead of setting nourishing, affirming standards, we hold ourselves to impossible heights (or none at all). None of this feels good or nourishing. Or remotely compassionate. Few of us fail to notice this behavior in others, but it can be tough to see or root out in ourselves.

According to self-compassion researcher Kristin Neff, one of the most important steps in finding compassion for yourself is to be mindful of your own suffering and able to be moved by it. Too often, though, being aware of how we're suffering unleashes a whole lot more self-judgment.

One way to shift that is to make a commitment to yourself that you will always have your own back.

If there's a lesson to learn or a wrong to right, you'll do that, too, but you will stand with yourself, no matter what. After all, that's what you'd do for your best friend or your child.

Whether you screw up or succeed, you stand with yourself.

When you can't get it all done and when you do, you stand with yourself.

When you handle it perfectly and when you don't, you stand with yourself.

I love this as a mindfulness practice. It's perfect for separating who we are from the external circumstances and bringing conscious awareness to how we might be suffering. Even better, it brings kindness and compassion right alongside.

Your 15-minute challenge:

Reflect on a recent situation that felt stressful. What did you need in that moment to feel compassionate support for yourself?

Now reflect on a recent success. What would a compassionate you do to acknowledge and celebrate that win?

Commit: I stand with myself. Always.

Daily Dare #19:
Take one small risk

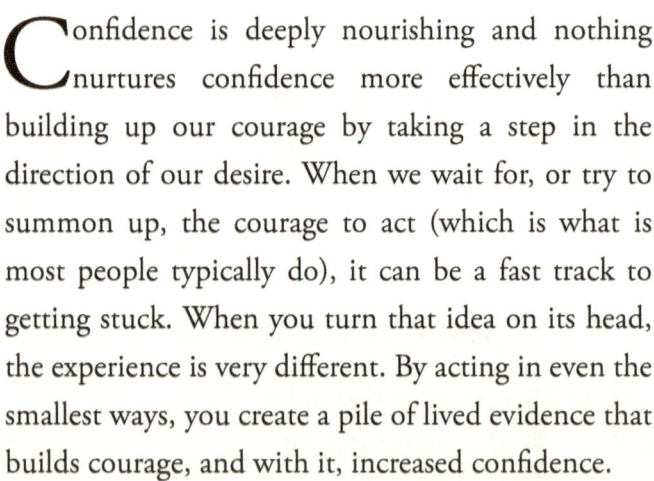

Confidence is deeply nourishing and nothing nurtures confidence more effectively than building up our courage by taking a step in the direction of our desire. When we wait for, or try to summon up, the courage to act (which is what is most people typically do), it can be a fast track to getting stuck. When you turn that idea on its head, the experience is very different. By acting in even the smallest ways, you create a pile of lived evidence that builds courage, and with it, increased confidence.

When you act with courage and confidence every day—and grant yourself the trust that you can do that even when it feels uncomfortable or unfamiliar—you create an entirely new level of self-care.

Here's what happens when you allow that confidence is accessible through action:

- You start speaking up when you have something important to share, instead of staying quiet.

- You ask for what you most want.

- You experiment with new perspectives and expand your possibilities.

- You feel good because you're acting with integrity and authenticity.

It's often said that everything you want lies on the other side of your comfort zone. I'd argue that it is you that lies on the other side of your comfort zone. Your truest self. The nourished, balanced, fulfilled, happy version of yourself at your authentic best.

Build up your courage capacity by nudging yourself from waiting to action. Your steps can be as small or as big as feels right for you right now. Just be sure to act in the direction of something that is meaningful for you.

Your 15-minute challenge:

Do one thing that stretches you out of your comfort zone, but that you know you can do (and just haven't done yet). Or choose to do one small thing that scares you. Consider doing this once a week, making it a regular practice of meaningful self-care.

Comfort zone expanders to try:

Daily Dare #20:
Cultivate positive feelings

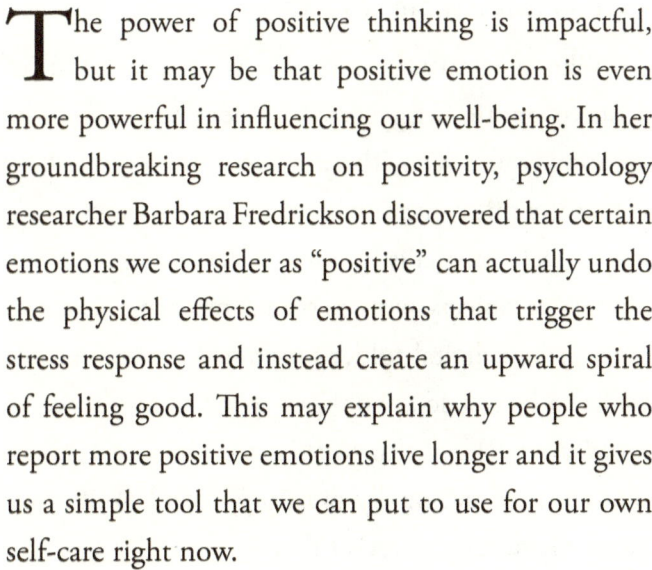

The power of positive thinking is impactful, but it may be that positive emotion is even more powerful in influencing our well-being. In her groundbreaking research on positivity, psychology researcher Barbara Fredrickson discovered that certain emotions we consider as "positive" can actually undo the physical effects of emotions that trigger the stress response and instead create an upward spiral of feeling good. This may explain why people who report more positive emotions live longer and it gives us a simple tool that we can put to use for our own self-care right now.

The "positive" emotions that Fredrickson studied were joy, gratitude, serenity, interest, hope, pride, amusement, inspiration, awe, and love. We hear a lot about gratitude because it's so well-documented that feeling thankful and taking actions that share and enhance that feeling improves self-reported well-being, but that's just one of 10 emotions that you can put to work for you.

One fun way to actively cultivate more positive emotions is to pay attention to the activities, objects, people, and situations that tend to trigger you to experience a specific emotion and then to curate them so that you can call on them when needed.

Like a gratitude journal, your collection of positive emotion triggers is a garden for growing the emotion you select. There are no rules about how you create this collection or what you may include. It might include emails, photos, letters, songs, quotes, videos, or objects with personal meaning. It could be kept in a digital folder on your desktop, in a file folder, a box, a scrapbook, on your smartphone, or on an altar. The goal is to collect a group of artifacts that are each personally meaningful and uplift your heart whenever you revisit them.

I've built these emotion collections myself in Dr. Fredrickson's class and loved the process so much that I use it with my clients and also included it here.

While 15 minutes isn't enough time to fully enjoy the process of building your collections, you can start. I encourage scheduling time to do more later.

Your 15-minute challenge:

Choose one of the 10 positive emotions that you'd like to feel more of. Brainstorm 10 creative ways that you can cultivate that emotion. Which one can you do today?

Find something that elicits that emotion in you today and take a photo with your phone. Keep a collection of these photos in an easily accessible album so you can pull them up as needed.

A positive emotion to cultivate is _____ .

10 ways to cultivate that emotion:

Daily Dare #21:
Connect

We all know how energizing and rewarding it can be to connect with somebody on a deeper level. It's also often the thing that we neglect to do when we're stretched too thin.

Yet the quality of our everyday relationships is a critical piece of our self-care. In fact, an 80-year study at Harvard found that close relationships—marital, familial, and social—are what keep people happy and healthy throughout their lives. Connecting, they found, buoys our mood even when we are stressed or in pain. And it helps to delay mental and physical decline and is a better predictor of long and happy lives than social class, IQ, or even genes.

While this study was done with men, I'd venture to say that many of us women are even more social creatures, with our "tend and befriend" nature. Building relationships happens over time, but it starts with something simple that you can do every single day without spending a lot of time. Connecting with others in an intentionally positive way makes you feel good, eases stress, and supports one of the most important steps we can take towards flourishing now and into the future.

Today, dare to make the effort to connect, even in the shortest of your interactions, and feel how that changes your experience of the day—and eventually enhances all of your relationships.

Your 15-minute challenge:

Today, stretch yourself to find three opportunities to really connect with people as you go through your day, whether at home, at work, in your community, or virtually.

Greet these people with warmth and respect and freely offer your attention. Make it a safe space to share authentic, lighthearted thoughts or feelings. Be present through eye contact, conversation or, when appropriate, touch. Do this in a way that feels natural and easy to you.

Record anything noteworthy about your response—or theirs.

Reflections on authentic connections:

FOUNDATION FOUR: ENVIRONMENT

Create a winning environment

It can be all too easy to go off-track with your putting your goals, dreams, and visions into action when they're not grounded in the life you live every day. If you've ever set a New Year's resolution in January only to be derailed by March, you know exactly how that works.

One of the most important factors contributing to this is the environment that we're operating within. By environments, we are talking about more than just physical spaces where we live and work. In addition to your physical living space and your office or workspace, there are many other influencing environmental factors to consider. Your overall environment includes the culture of your workplace, the relationships you spend time in, your work and home schedule, your commitments, your community, the digital or online spaces where you spend time, your finances, and more.

As we make changes to support sustainable self-care for our mind, body, and spirit, we may have trouble maintaining those changes and self-care routines when the environment around us doesn't support our new change but instead remains the same. The question we need to ask next is, "What are the adjustments I need to make to my environments to support and enable my nourishing practices?"

An early mentor of mine once shared with me a piece of advice that I took to heart at the time and that I have held close ever since: your environment always wins. What she meant by this is that the various environments we operate in have a huge influence on how we think, what we do, the results we get and, of course, on our general well-being. Environmental factors can, in fact, make it harder to practice good self-care. They can hold you back if you allow them to, or they can support you.

That doesn't mean that you're fated to be a victim of who and what is around you, although some of us do pretend that's true. It's a call to take charge of the environments that you choose to operate within and how you, as an adult of free will, can start to make changes where needed in order to build a supportive environment around you.

As you start to evaluate your environment, you may find that there are changes you can make that serve as natural nudges toward choosing the nourishment that you crave, such as ensuring that your kitchen is filled with healthy food options or keeping a book of inspirational reading by your bed. You might also make environmental adjustments that protect you from distracting or triggering influences, such as setting boundaries around digital spaces or evaluating where you spend the most time.

By continually tweaking your environment to support and foster your desired self-care practices, you set yourself up for easier and more lasting success. You may also find that once you start challenging yourself to own your environment as your choice, it becomes a healthy addiction. Improvements in one area nearly always lead to improvements in other areas, creating a virtuous upward spiral. They can also serve as a positive influence on others who share your environments.

These final seven days of your Nourish challenge are key to your ongoing self-care success. This is where you're going to stretch yourself to experiment with actions that will enhance your environments and allow them to better support you in nurturing your mind, body, and spirit. Creating a sustainable practice of nourishing and caring for your whole self gets a whole lot easier when you are committed to setting up a network of environments that will support you in that mission. Consider the possibility that you can, over time and with work, establish beautifully supportive environments all around you!

You'll have seven different environmental adjustments to play with this week, all of which are designed to help you explore which aspects of your own environments would best support you in developing a more naturally nourishing support system all around you.

If your environment is going to win, let's be sure that you share the same goals and that you are winning right along with it!

5 ENVIRONMENTAL CHANGES TO CONSIDER THIS WEEK

I set solid boundaries around my time and energy commitments.

I am sprucing up my physical environment so that it nourishes and pleases me.

I commit to seeking support where and when I need that.

I surround myself with inspiration, not drama.

I prioritize taking care of unfinished business or draining situations.

Daily Dare #22:
Let's get visual

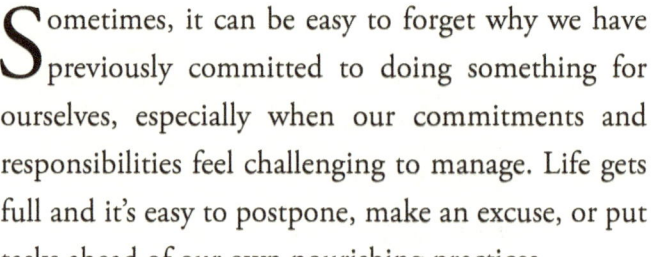

Sometimes, it can be easy to forget why we have previously committed to doing something for ourselves, especially when our commitments and responsibilities feel challenging to manage. Life gets full and it's easy to postpone, make an excuse, or put tasks ahead of our own nourishing practices.

Creating a visual reminder of why we're doing what we're doing can be incredibly effective. I employed this strategy when I first began strength training at a gym several years ago. Using bright colored Sharpies and a sheet of white paper, I listed all the reasons why I was making that decision, titled it Why I Work Out, and posted it on my kitchen wall.

Whenever I thought of a new reason, I added it to the list. Every morning, as I made my coffee, I couldn't miss seeing all those reasons why I work out. All these years later, while I no longer have that list, the environment that it created resulted in a nourishing habit that has stuck.

Think about why you picked up this book. Why was it important for you to spend time on strategies to nourish your body, mind, spirit, and environment? Look around your environment. What are the visual cues that you notice? Where might you incorporate a visual cue to help you fully integrate your favorite nourishing practices?

When your environment visually supports your self-care needs and desires, you'll be more likely to integrate those practices into your daily life and build upon them.

Your 15-minute challenge:

Pull out a piece of paper and colorful pens, if you've got them. Jot down a list of 10 reasons that taking the time for easy, simple, self-care every day matters to you. Next, list 10 simple things that nourish you.

Post these lists where you will see them every

single day. Or take photos and keep them on your phone. Create a beautiful graphic. Get creative with ways to ensure that you are visually reminded of the why and the what.

For an extra challenge, adjust something else in your visual environment to support your most nourishing version of self-care.

Daily Dare #23:
Draw your lines

Your lines are the places where your boundaries, standards, and values intersect. To draw them in a nourishing way requires intentionality. It requires you to make decisions about where you are willing to commit, and what you are willing to prioritize among the many internal and external forces that are vying for your attention, energy, or time.

This is how you take a stand for your bigger picture vision and stand in fuller sovereignty over your life. Clear lines help you to define what matters to you, identify and give yourself what you need to be your best, and gain clarity about what you will and will not create or allow in your life.

Drawing a line is always about you, not anyone else. It's not about controlling outside circumstances, but about setting your own standards and priorities. This is where you make your values and priorities truly count by putting them into consistent practice.

Your lines are joyful and life-affirming. They're the engines of your day. They're about who you're being as well as what you're doing. They're about what you are saying yes to and what is a no. Here are just a few of the benefits of drawing your lines effectively:

- *Decision-making framework*—You move forward faster and say no easier with clear standards.

- *Empowerment*—When you've made the rules, you can follow them or change them.

- *Focused energy*—When you know what works for you, you naturally default to that.

- *No drama*—When you set clear parameters, you know what meets them and what doesn't.

Consider trying out this decision-making filter when thinking about where your lines need to be right now:

It's an easy yes. If it's truly a yes for you, go all in and be present for it. If what you're thinking about doing is not worth that kind of commitment and attention, then it's worth rethinking why you're saying yes.

Thank you, but no thank you. Making room a true, committed yes usually requires saying no to something else. For example, it's fine to say, "No, I don't have time this week for everything on my list," or, "No, I don't want to do that." No to what's not in the highest good of you, the people in your life and the commitments you've made. No to drama and things that feel off to you. That leaves much more room for "yes" and "thank you."

Your 15-minute challenge:

Today, identify one or two lines that you'd like to draw to help you to feel more nourished, grounded, and balanced. Experiment with the stand that you'd like to take in these areas.

Boundary lines to draw include:

Daily Dare #24:

One-step sanctuary

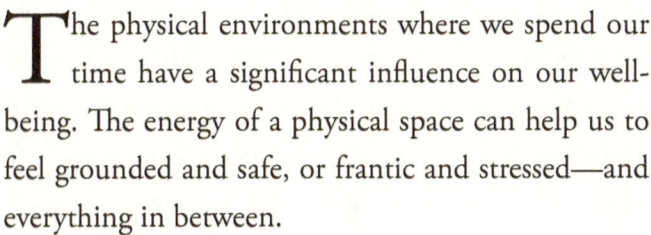

The physical environments where we spend our time have a significant influence on our well-being. The energy of a physical space can help us to feel grounded and safe, or frantic and stressed—and everything in between.

Think about the spaces in which you love to spend your time, the places where you feel at home, where you feel at ease, comfortable, and nourished. Maybe it's your favorite café, a park you like to visit, a dear friend's house, or a corner of your own home. What makes those spaces feel good to you? What are the physical attributes of those spaces that give you energy?

Now, think about the spaces that have the opposite effect on you. What are the attributes of these spaces that drain your energy?

For example, I feel most relaxed and at home in physical environments that are reasonably organized, clean, bright, and calm. The energy I feel in these kinds of spaces fuels me in a way that cluttered and dark spaces cannot, so I've turned the sunniest room in my home into my home office. I am not just talking about living and working environments here; anywhere we spend time and energy has a demonstrated impact on our well-being, so choose wisely.

Making simple and small changes to the places where we spend our time can have a profound impact on how we feel, act, and perform in those spaces. If you know that you work best in an organized, bright, and clean office, for example, taking five minutes to clear off your desk at the end of the day, using great lighting, and having a simple file system are tiny investments with a big payoff.

Your 15-minute challenge:

What's one thing that you can adjust in your home environment today to make it feel more nourishing to you?

What's one thing you can do at work today to make your workspace more nourishing?

Do them both.

For an extra challenge, make a list below and during the next week try adjusting one thing per day so that your environments feel more supportive.

A more supportive home environment looks like this:

_____

_____

_____

_____

_____

_____

_____

A more supportive work environment looks like this:

_____

_____

_____

_____

_____

_____

_____

Daily Dare #25:
Intentional inputs

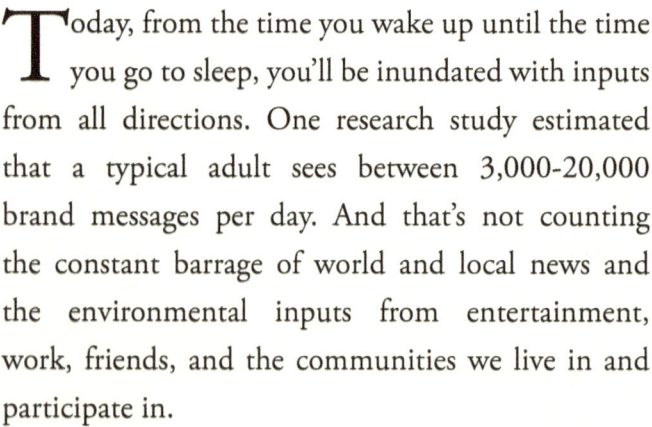

Today, from the time you wake up until the time you go to sleep, you'll be inundated with inputs from all directions. One research study estimated that a typical adult sees between 3,000-20,000 brand messages per day. And that's not counting the constant barrage of world and local news and the environmental inputs from entertainment, work, friends, and the communities we live in and participate in.

Everyone is vying for our attention and we all have a limited amount of time, energy, and mental bandwidth every day. Depending on what's happening in your world, that bandwidth may be wider or more limited.

One strategy for managing external inputs that can have far-reaching effects on our well-being is to be intentional about what we let in. Intentional input is about choosing what you're allowing in and when you decide to do that. This requires setting clear boundaries and exercising a measure of control over your immediate world.

Maybe instead of the news, you tune in to music that you love. Instead of starting your day with social media or email, you choose 15 minutes of inspiring reading, quiet time, or getting a quick but important task accomplished.

Managing your inputs might mean giving up the news, violent films or late-night crime shows for something that feels better. Perhaps you need to turn off your phone or answer emails only twice a day. Or maybe it's time to unsubscribe from social media notifications or email lists that are draining and distracting you.

Pay attention to what you let into your environment and how you feel when you engage with those things.

Your 15-minute challenge:

Today, take 15 minutes to reconsider what you're letting in that might be working against your self-care strategies.

Opt out from one or more of those things today. Replace it with something more nourishing.

Inputs that are not nourishing

_____

_____

_____

_____

_____

_____

Nourishing replacements

_____

_____

_____

_____

_____

_____

_____

Daily Dare #26:
Build your backups + buffers

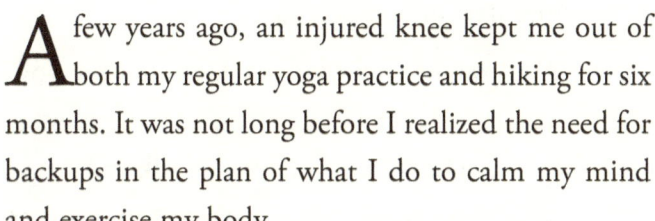

A few years ago, an injured knee kept me out of both my regular yoga practice and hiking for six months. It was not long before I realized the need for backups in the plan of what I do to calm my mind and exercise my body.

After whining about how I could not do "anything," I made a backup plan. I started walking in the park and doing upper body weights. It worked. My body was moving and my mind was clearer, and I discovered new activities that I enjoy and maintain. What I learned is this: sometimes your go-to plan is just not possible, but you can always find another nourishing choice. You might even grow to value it on its own merits.

Having backups and buffers is a great strategy for nourishing all parts of our lives. A backup ensures that circumstances don't throw us off track or into less-than-nourishing habits, especially when we have worked to establish solid self-care practices. A buffer puts space between us and the situation that could cause stress. Here are a few ways they can be implemented:

- You might choose to add buffers of time in your schedule between appointments or at the start or end of a day.

- You might consider stocking up on your favorite or most often used toiletries or pantry items. Can you buy in bulk and keep a reserve on hand to avoid last-minute panics?

- You might build an emergency fund as a financial buffer against unexpected expenses or job changes.

- You could have a backup plan for when a late meeting or the weather changes your workout or healthy dinner plans.

Systematically building buffers and backups into your life is a wonderful way to design less stress and more simplicity into your daily life. It may take a little thought and organization at first, but once you start thinking this way, you will feel even more supported and taken care of in your life.

Where would a backup or a buffer ensure that your self-care needs are met?

Your 15-minute challenge:

Start building some buffers and backups into your environment. Choose one area where having a buffer would feel supportive. Strategize how you can make that happen this week.

Then, make a list of everywhere you'd like to have a buffer or a backup. You can make that list happen over time. Just getting it on paper will have you brainstorming "buffers and backups" everywhere!

Places that I can install backup plans and buffers into my life include:

_____

_____

_____

_____

_____

Daily Dare #27:
Financial self-care

There are plenty of resources and supports to help you manage your money and even examine your personal relationship to money, which can be a loaded symbol in many cultures. Choosing to take ownership of your financial resources is also a very practical piece of foundational self-care. Making that choice is far less about your relationship to money than to your relationship with yourself.

Most of us infuse our financial lives with a lot of baggage and responsibility that it doesn't necessarily warrant. Money is a necessary tool for us to use and manage in order to live in the society that we inhabit, not the other way around. Let's examine your financial situation for a moment and see where more nourishment may be possible.

What needs to be taken care of for you to feel that you are financially nourished?

Where do you currently feel nourished by your finances?

Where is your financial life making you feel stressed instead of nourished?

What would meaningful financial self-care look like to you?

How might you allocate your resources towards creating a fully nourished life?

As with many of the strategies that we're exploring in this course, financial self-care is an ongoing practice—and for some of us it requires a significant mindset shift. Today, we'll start small and simple with one step. I encourage and invite you, though, to make that one step a significant one.

Your 15-minute challenge:

What would truly represent a step towards financial nourishment for you? Today, you'll take one step towards making that happen. One concrete step. Maybe it's:

- Funding a dream or an activity you wish to nourish in your life

- Opening an investment account

- Balancing (or looking at!) your accounts

- Understanding your net worth

- Paying an overdue bill

- Assigning a percentage of your money to a purpose that is meaningful to you

- Making a date to sort records that have gotten out of hand

- Creating a nourishing spending plan or scheduling a date to do that

- Letting go of finances as an excuse for letting self-care lag (as you now know, it doesn't need to cost anything)

- Designating a financial independence or retirement number to work towards

How will you prioritize your financial self-care going forward?

Daily Dare #28:
Do a values audit

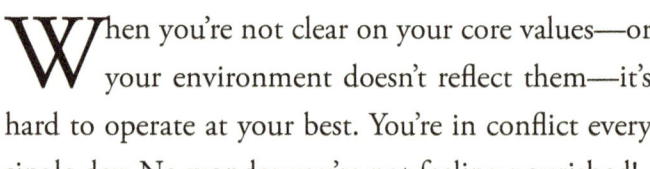

When you're not clear on your core values—or your environment doesn't reflect them—it's hard to operate at your best. You're in conflict every single day. No wonder you're not feeling nourished!

Your values are the preferences, situations, and activities that are so ingrained in who you are that you just could not be your best without them. These are the things that you naturally gravitate towards throughout your life. They are, in essence, you. Creating an environment around you in which these values are honored fuels everything you do.

And yet, many people try to fit like round pegs in square holes, instead of intentionally crafting environments around them to fit with who they are and what matters to them. Today, you're going to move towards bringing the two together by seeing where your values and your environments intersect and where they don't yet.

It might be that you value family, and so a work schedule that impinges on your family time is going to quickly exhaust you and feel misaligned. Or maybe freedom is a core value and you need to design your financial life or work life to allow more autonomy and choice. Maybe you value creativity but you aren't creating.

It might be that you need time with animals or in nature. Maybe it's beauty, and your garden offers that. Influence, adventure, calm, contribution, impact—your values mix is different and unique to you. But we're all at our best when we're continually refining our environments to reflect and honor what deeply matters to us.

Your 15-minute challenge:

Brainstorm your top three to five values. Chances are, you've learned a lot about what truly matters to you in the last few weeks, so start there.

How could the environment around you (your physical space, schedule, relationships, mental space) be more aligned with these values? Commit to making one of those changes in the next week, if not today.

PART

3

CREATING YOUR NOURISH PLAN

What's possible now?

Congratulations! I hope that you are feeling more nourished as you've experimented with ways to take excellent care of your mind, body, and spirit, and begin to curate your tangible and intangible environments to support you being at your best.

Over the past 28 days, you've explored:

- Time-tested ways to quiet your mind and hear your own voice

- Simple strategies to nourish your body every

day, without it feeling like a chore

- Creative ways to feed your spirit

- Where you might need to set stronger boundaries to support your well-being.

- What fuels you and what doesn't

- How taking even a few tiny moments for yourself each day can be a game-changer

- How to nourish yourself, in your way, on your schedule

- Why self-care is more a process of committing to your full well-being and less about treating yourself (although treats are important, too!)

In life and career coaching, we often use personal strategic plans and maps to ground our vision in reality. A vision sets the agenda and the plan helps us take the consistent daily steps, do the inner work and establish the consistency needed to live into that vision.

To create your own foundational Nourish Plan, I invite you to step back into your experience of the last 28 days and revisit your favorite and most resonant Daily Dares. What particularly resonated with you, touched on something you were needing, or felt the most fun to do? To naturally create balance in your plan, you'll want to ensure that you're nourishing all the parts of your foundation. Select at least one practice from each of the Mind, Body, Spirit, and Environment modules to create the basis of your own Nourish Plan going forward.

Remember to start small and harness the power of micro-actions. You can always add more later, once you've had a chance to fully integrate these most desired actions into your daily life. I'm confident that you will want to build on your plan once you've integrated these first practices, but there's no need to rush that.

A few tips:

Be sure to choose only activities or habits that you want to do regularly, not the ones you think you should be doing or that you believe will get you a certain result.

Adjust and adapt any practice as you see fit. Allow it to enhance your lifestyle, your schedule, and your goals. The Daily Dares are meant to get you experimenting!

Check in with yourself regularly. What's feeling most challenging? What's been a natural fit? What's evolving for you? What gives you a feeling of deep nourishment?

When it's time to add more, start at the top with a mindset practice and add one practice per foundational area at a time. This will help to keep your self-care integrated and naturally balanced. You may want to select practices that have the greatest impact on your well-being.

Don't forget to celebrate and savor this big commitment you have made to nourishing your own mind, body, and spirit—and to actively setting up your environment to support the life that you are creating for yourself. That's a huge part of feeling truly nourished in your life. The more we take care of ourselves, the more we inspire others to do the same. The more we are nourished, the more we are able to live our most fulfilled, balanced, happiest lives. Our capacity to serve and contribute grows. With that in mind, consider sharing what you've learned. Choose one creative way to share and celebrate your accomplishment with someone else. (You can even send them this book!)

Imagine what becomes possible for all of us when we are all truly paying attention to and meeting our most important needs and nourishing ourselves at a deep level.

Your Nourish Plan

"When you recover or discover something that nourishes your soul and brings joy, care enough about yourself to make room for it in your life."

- Jean Shinoda Bolen

To create your foundational plan, choose one or two Daily Dares from each of the four foundation areas that you will commit to implementing regularly in your life, starting now. Remember to choose practices that will be easy to integrate into your schedule, that you want to do (no shoulds!), and that you know will have an impact for you. Start small and focus on consistency first.

Once you've selected your foundation, note any other practices that have worked well for you over the last 28 days or those that you haven't tried but want to experiment with. These will be your next steps. As you develop your own unique blend of nourishment for your mind, body, spirit, and environment, you can dip back into the book for more ideas and come up with your own ways of incorporating these 28 strategies into your life.

Mind

_____

_____

_____

_____

Body

_____

_____

_____

_____

Spirit

_____

_____

_____

_____

Environment

_____

_____

_____

_____

Other practices that have worked well:

_____

_____

_____

_____

_____

_____

_____

_____

_____

_____

Practices to experiment with:

_____

_____

_____

_____

_____

_____

_____

_____

What's next?

You've done the hard work, and now you're well on the path to creating sustainable self-care practices that work for your busy life. I'd love to hear about what has resonated most with you, what's become a part of your Nourish Plan, and what you're currently celebrating.

As you move forward with integrating your Nourish Plan into your daily life, read the Whole Life Strategies blog for new tools, inspiration, accountability, encouragement, obstacle-tackling, and mindset shifts.

Get bimonthly tips, resources, and insights delivered to your inbox.

You can always reach out for help, too. If you'd like to discuss ongoing individual coaching to help you manage your energy and revitalize your life and work, let's talk.

You can find it all and stay connected here:

www.wholelifestrategies.com

References and Further Reading

Duhigg, C. (2012). The power of habit: Why we do what we do in life and business. New York, NY: Random House.

Gino, F. (2013). Sidetracked: Why our decisions get derailed, and how we can stick to the plan. Boston, MA: Harvard Business Review.

Kim, S.H. (2014). Evidence-based advice for college students: Microaction and macrochange. The Mentor: An Academic Advising Journal.

McDonough, K. (2013, January 2). Study: You're probably going to break your New Year's resolution. Salon. Retrieved from https://www.salon.com/2013/01/02/study_youre_probably_going_to_break_your_new_years_resolution/

Rubin, G. (2009, August 28). Make your bed. Retrieved from The Happiness Project website: http://www.happiness-project.com/

Thaler, R. H., & Sunstein, C. R. (2008). Nudge: Improving decisions about health, wealth, and happiness. New York, NY: Penguin Books

Mineo, Liz (2017, April 11) Good genes are nice, but joy is better. The Harvard Gazette. Retrieved from: https://news.harvard.edu/gazette/story/2017/04/over-nearly-80-years-harvard-study-has-been-showing-how-to-live-a-healthy-and-happy-life/

Harvard Study of Adult Development. Retrieved from https://www.adultdevelopmentstudy.org.

Fredrickson, Barbara. Positive Emotions and Psychophysiology Laboratory, University of North Carolina at Chapel Hill. https://peplab.web.unc.edu

Hanson, Rick (2013) Hardwiring Happiness: The new brain science of contentment, calm and confidence. Harmony.

Neff, Kristen (2011) Self-Compassion: Stop beating yourself up and leave insecurity behind. William Morrow.

Gratitude

Learning how to experiment with and dial in a solid foundation of self-care has involved a lot of learning, experimentation and in some cases, trial by fire. I owe much to the many teachers I've studied with over the last 20 years, from coaching and self-development to mindfulness, from creative pursuits to business.

I also owe gratitude to the many women and men who have shared their stories, struggles, and celebrations about what it means to meaningfully nourish themselves and revitalize their lives throughout my years of coaching them through life and career reinventions. Together, your experiences and mine have formed the ideas that made me want to write this book.

To the many friends, family members, and colleagues who taught me firsthand what it means to step back and nourish myself when times are challenging and the impact that can have on resilience and sustainability. You know who you are and I love you all.

To Michael, my partner in life, adventures, and real-life balance for your perspective, boundless energy, unwavering encouragement, and drive to do life your way.

To Cheryl, for teaching me more about what self-care is and is not at a time when I most needed to learn that, and for modeling how much that evolves throughout our lives.

About Sally

Sally Anne Carroll is a life and career reinvention coach and the founder of Whole Life Strategies Coaching and Artisan Communications. She supports motivated professionals and entrepreneurs who crave, or are facing, significant changes in their life or career to reinvent their reality so that they're living and working in a way that matches their values, strengths, needs, and priorities. As a reinvention strategist and coach, Sally is known as a fierce advocate for designing lifestyles and careers that work together in a balanced, vibrant, and intentional way—and provide more of what matters every day. She fervently believes that is possible for all of us— and that truly nourishing self-care is the foundation.

She is a graduate of Boston University, a professional credentialed coach with the International Coach Federation (ICF) and holds multiple coaching credentials in modalities including applied positive psychology coaching, narrative coaching, neuroscience-based coaching interventions, career invention coaching, mindfulness, and others.

Sally lives a balanced life of her own design with her partner in reinvention and in life, splitting time between Oregon and New Zealand. When not coaching or writing, often she can be found out in nature, in her backyard garden, getting into a good book, cooking up a new recipe, or planning travel adventures.

Stay connected with Sally, get strategic support for creating sustainable success, and share your celebrations and your feedback on this book here:

www.sallyannecarroll.com

www.wholelifestrategies.com